Oxford Phonics World 4
Consonant Blends

Kaj Schwermer   Julia Chang   Craig Wright

OXFORD
UNIVERSITY PRESS

Consonant Blends

Unit 1   bl cl br cr fl gl 4

     bl cl .... black blanket clock club
     br cr .... broom bride crab crocodile
     fl gl .... fly flag globe glass
     Story 11

Unit 2   fr gr pl sl dr tr 12

     fr gr .... frog Friday green grass
     pl sl .... plate play slide sleep
     dr tr .... drum dress truck tree
     Story 19

Review 1   **Song** ♪ 20
              Game 23

Unit 3   sm sn sp sw st 24

     sm sn .... smile smoke snake snow
     sp sw .... spoon spot swing swim
     st .... stop test stamp fast
     Story 31

Unit 4   sh ch tch ph wh 32

     sh .... shell fish ship brush
     ch tch .... chick lunch watch catch
     ph wh .... phone dolphin whale white
     Story 39

Review 2   **Song** ♪ 40
              Game 43

Unit 5 $\quad$ ^voiced^th $\quad$ ^unvoiced^th $\quad$ ck qu 44

- voiced th ...... this that mother father
- unvoiced th ... three teeth think bath
- ck qu .... duck rocket queen quilt
- **Story** 51

Unit 6 $\quad$ ng nk nd nt lt mp 52

- ng nk .... king long bank pink
- nd nt .... wind hand tent paint
- lt mp .... belt adult lamp camp
- **Story** 59

Review 3 **Song** 60
$\qquad\qquad$ **Game** 63

Unit 7 $\quad$ sk sc spr str spl squ 64

- sk sc .... skunk desk scale school
- spr str .... spray spring string strong
- spl squ .... splash splint squid square
- **Story** 71

Unit 8 $\quad$ ^soft^c ^soft^g ^voiced^s 72

- soft c .... rice city ice cream cell phone
- soft g .... giraffe orange giant cage
- voiced s ...... rose jeans cheese legs
- **Story** 79

Review 4 **Song** 80
$\qquad\qquad$ **Game** 83

Picture Dictionary 84
Student Cards 89
Certificate 101

Unit 1 — bl cl br cr fl gl

A Listen and learn. *disc 1 03*

b + l = bl
black

c + l = cl
clock

B Listen, point, and read. *disc 1 04*

1. black
2. blanket
3. clock
4. club

C Listen, read, and match.

1. clock / club
2. blanket / blue
3. club / blanket
4. clue / black

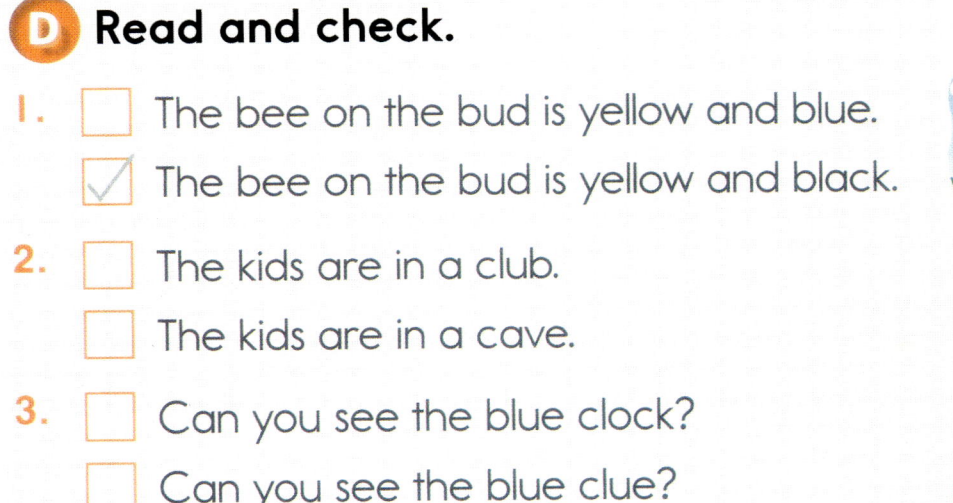

D Read and check.

1. ☐ The bee on the bud is yellow and blue.
   ☑ The bee on the bud is yellow and black.
2. ☐ The kids are in a club.
   ☐ The kids are in a cave.
3. ☐ Can you see the blue clock?
   ☐ Can you see the blue clue?
4. ☐ I have a black coat.
   ☐ I have a black blanket.

E Listen and chant. Then read.

Our club has a blue clock and a black blanket.

Unit 1 5

bl cl br cr fl gl

A Listen and learn. disc 1 07

b + r = br
b r o o m

c + r = cr
c r a b

B Listen, point, and read. disc 1 08

1.  broom
2.  bride
3.  crab
4.  crocodile

Unit 1

C Which ones have the same sounds? Listen and circle. disc 1 09

D Listen and circle. Then write. disc 1 10

1. cr / ab / ocodile — crab
2. br oom / ide
3. bl anket / ack
4. cr ab / ocodile
5. cl ock / ub
6. br ide / oom

E Listen and chant. Then read. disc 1 11

 The bride wants a broom, a crab, and a crocodile.

Unit 1 7

bl cl br cr fl gl

A Listen and learn.

f + l = f l

f l y

g + l = g l

g l o b e

B Listen, point, and read.

1. fly
2. flag
3. globe
4. glass

Unit 1

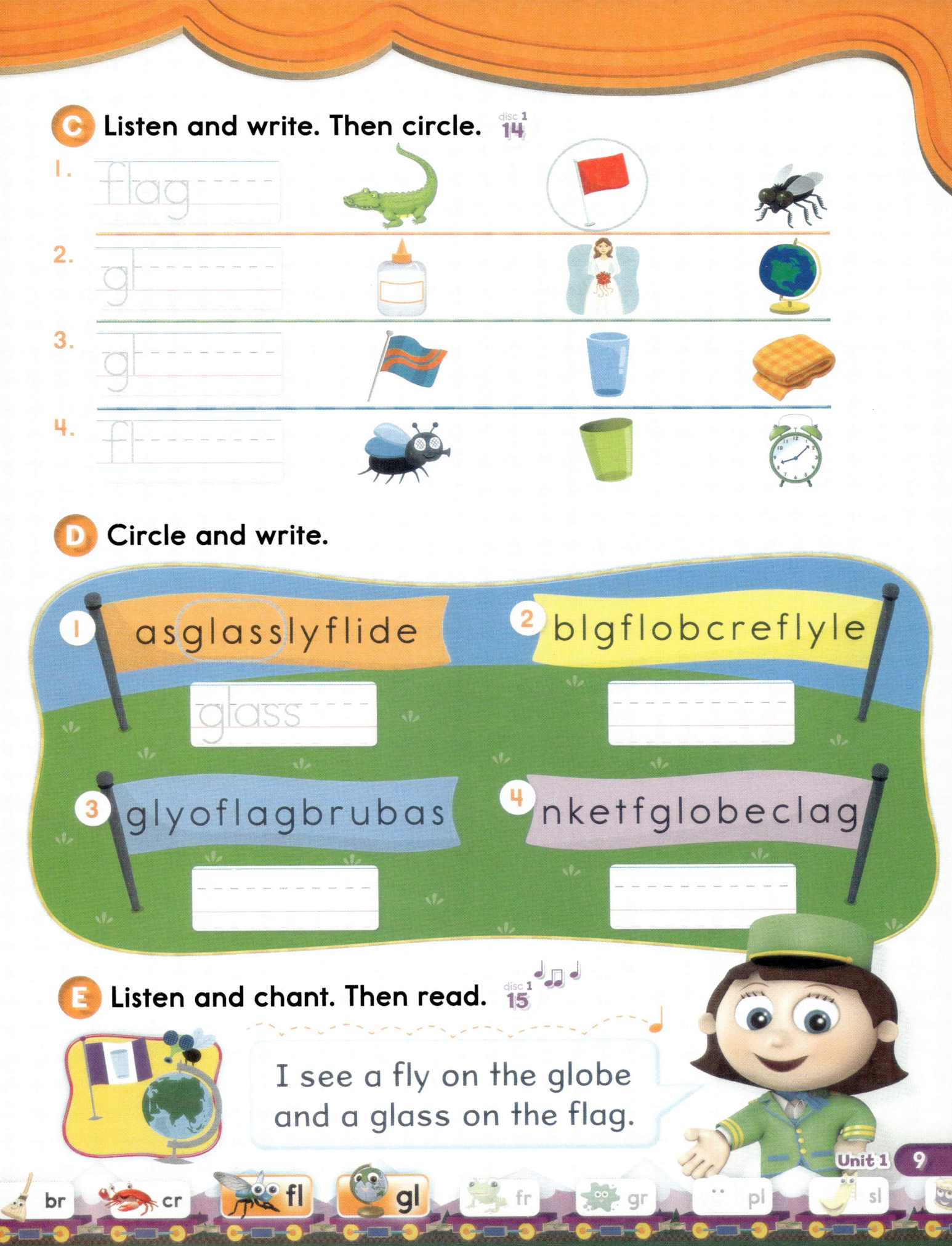

bl cl br cr fl gl

A Read and write.

~~clock~~ fly bride glass broom crocodile
black flag crab globe blanket club

bl cl fl gl | br cr

clock

Now try these! Listen, unscramble, and write.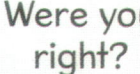

Were you right?

1. oklbc
   block

2. alnce

3. kbcri

4. earnc

5. utlef

6. lgedi

B Look and listen. Read along. *disc 1, 17*

Story

The Club

The fly, the crab, and the crocodile are friends. This is their club.

Our club is a mess. We need to clean up!

I can use the broom to sweep.

I can put away the blanket and put up the flag.

I can wipe the globe with a rag.

Now our club is clean!

Look at the clock. It's time to eat!

New words: mess sweep wipe   **Sight words:** their clean away it's

Unit 1

 br  cr  fl  gl  fr gr pl sl

Unit 2   fr gr pl sl dr tr

A Listen and learn. disc 1 18

f + r = fr
frog

g + r = gr
green

B Listen, point, and read. disc 1 19

1.
2.
3.
4.

frog   Friday   green   grass

 bl    cl    br 

fr gr pl sl dr tr

A Listen and learn. disc 1 · 22

p + l = pl
plate

s + l = sl
slide

B Listen, point, and read. disc 1 · 23

1. plate 2. play 3. slide 4. sleep

fr gr pl sl dr tr

A Listen and learn. disc 1 / 26

d + r = dr

d r u m

t + r = tr

t r u c k

B Listen, point, and read. disc 1 / 27

1. drum
2. dress
3. truck
4. tree

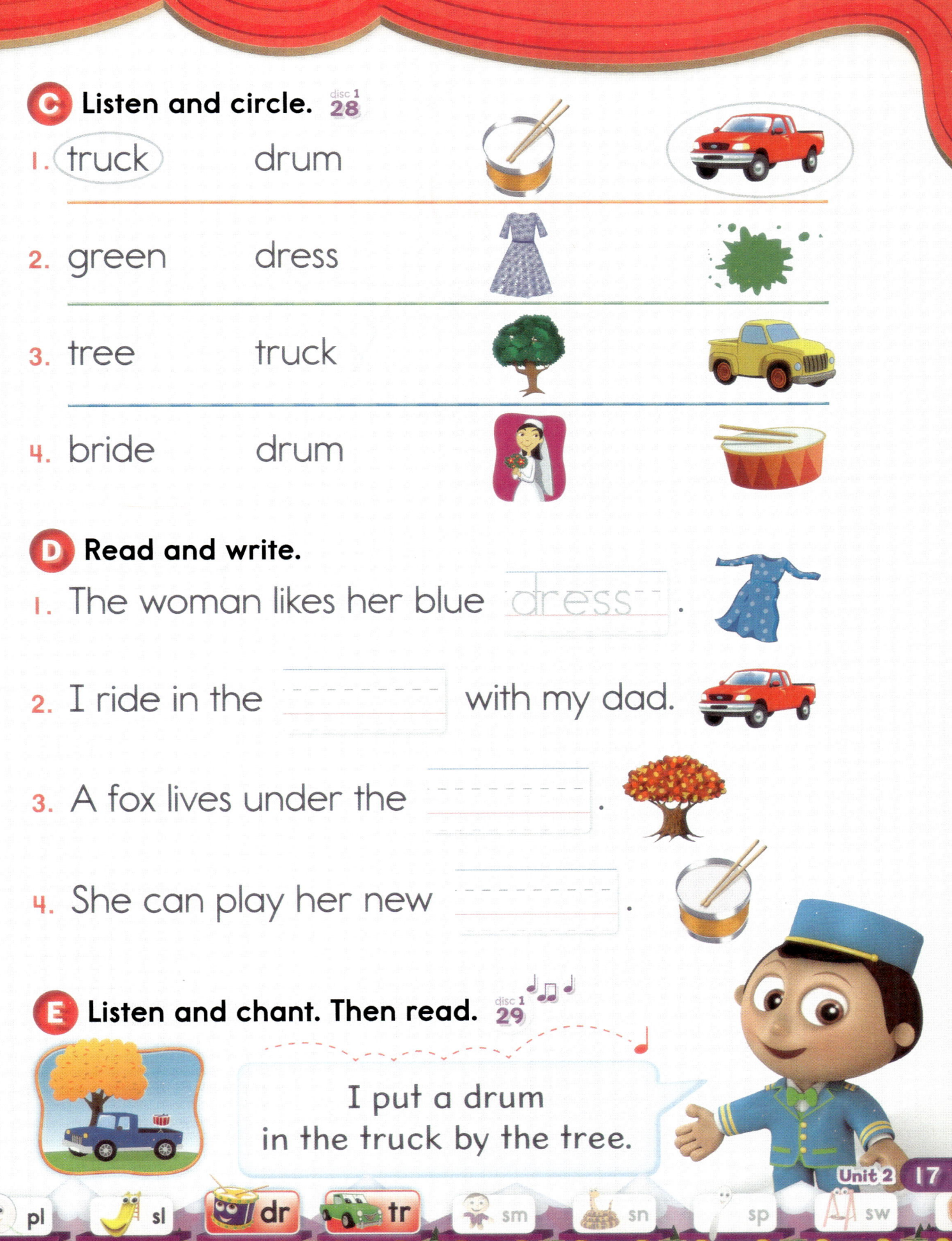

fr gr pl sl dr tr

A Listen and write. disc 1 30

fr gr dr tr   pl sl

green

Now try these! Listen and circle. disc 1 31

Were you right?

1. (sl)ow / gr
2. fl ame / fr
3. pl ain / tr
4. pl ug / sl
5. dr ape / gr
6. dr ink / bl

 bl  cl   br  cr  fl  gl  fr

Story

B Look and listen. Read along. disc 1 / 32

Happy Frogs

1. The green frogs live in a big tree.

2. On Friday, they drive their truck to the park. They bring a lot of food and plates.

3. Some frogs drum, and some frogs swim. They hop in the grass and play on the slide.

4. On Saturday, all the frogs sleep late!

New words: drive park Saturday late   Sight words: bring all

Unit 2

Review 1

bl cl br cr fl gl fr gr pl sl dr tr

A Look and listen. Sing along.

Song

It's Saturday. It's Saturday.
The kids go to the park and play.
She likes to go on the slide.
He likes to take a truck to ride.

They eat on a blanket on the grass.
He has a plate. She has a glass.
Mom and Dad, can you see
The bride under the big, green tree?

B Do the puzzle.

1.
2.
3.
4.
5.

Across:
1. bride
2. crocodile
3. glass
4. plate
5. sleep

Down:
6. truck
7. black
8. flag
9. dress
10. grass

6. 7. 8. 9. 10.

Review 1 21

 pl  sl  dr  tr  sm  sn sp  sw bl cl br cr fl gl fr gr pl sl dr tr

C Listen and circle.

1.
gl dr (pl)

2.
sl dr br

3.
fr br fl

4.
gr cl cr

5.
gl tr cr

6.
cl bl gr

D Match and write.

1. gr — obe
   gl — een
    green
    globe

2. sl — ide
   cl — ub

3. bl — oom
   br — anket

4. Fr — iday
   fl — y

Review 1

Game

E Play the game.

clock

green

dress

grass

End

crab

slide

globe

Friday

club

frog

sleep

black

crocodile

flag

plate

blanket

tree

play

broom

fly

glass

truck

bride

drum

Start

Review 1 23

Unit 3   sm sn sp sw st

A Listen and learn.

| s | + | m | = | s m |

smile

| s | + | n | = | s n |

snake

B Listen, point, and read.

1. smile
2. smoke
3. snake
4. snow

sm sn sp sw st

A Listen and learn. 🎧 39

| s | + | p | = | sp |

spoon

| s | + | w | = | sw |

swing

B Listen, point, and read. 🎧 40

1. 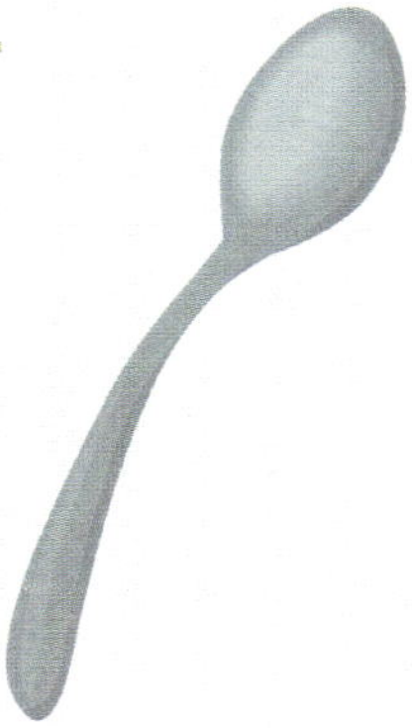 spoon
2.  spot
3.  swing
4.  swim

sm sn sp sw **st**

A Listen and learn.

s + t = **st**

stop

B Listen, point, and read.

1.
stop

2.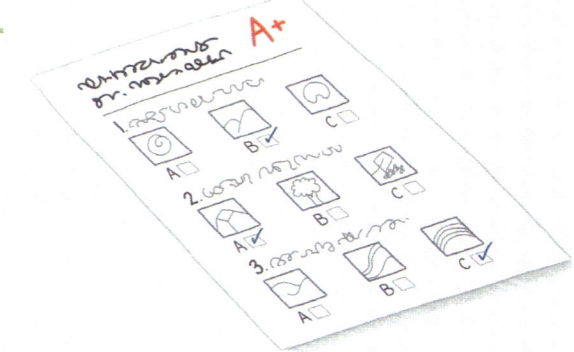
te**st**

3.
stamp

4.
fa**st**

sm sn sp sw st

A Read and write.

spot test smoke snow fast smile
stamp stop swing spoon snake swim

sm

sn

st

sp

sw

Now try these! Listen, unscramble, and write. disc 1 47

1. lmlse
2. sialn
3. esllp
4. peswe
5. osten
6. smit

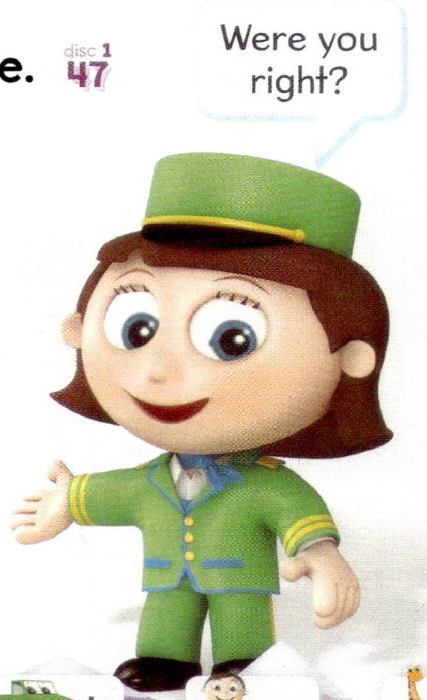

Were you right?

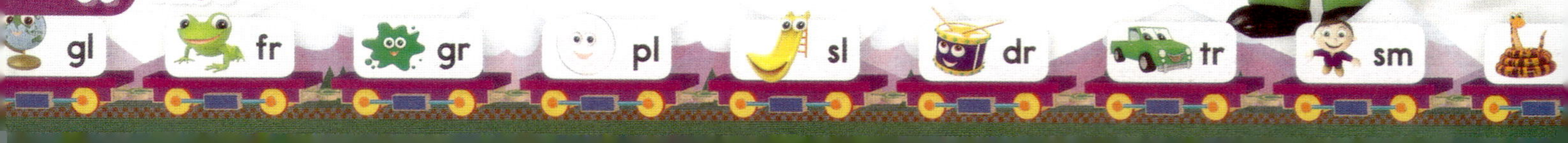

gl
fr
gr
pl
sl
dr
tr
sm

Story

B Look and listen. Read along.

Seasons

Hi, I'm Fran. In winter, my class takes a big test. Then we go on vacation!

We play outside in the snow. Some kids are fast on their skates. My friend and I smile. We make hot tea and stir it with a spoon.

In summer, we play outside in the sun! We swim in the lake and go on the swings.

I like the winter and the summer. What season do you like?

New words: seasons Fran vacation class outside tea stir summer
Sight words: I'm

Unit 4   sh ch tch ph wh

A Listen and learn. disc 1 49

shell

s h

B Listen, point, and read. disc 1 50

1.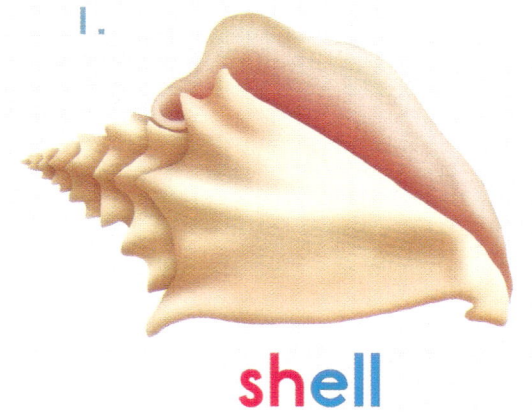
shell

2.
fish

3.
ship

4.
brush

sh ch tch ph wh

A Listen and learn. disc 1 / 54

chick
c h

watch
t c h

B Listen, point, and read. disc 1 / 55

1. chick
2. lunch
3. watch
4. catch

C Listen and number. Then match.

lunch ☐   chick ☐   catch ☐   watch ☐

D Unscramble and write.

1.
2.
3.
4.

thcca   hickc   lchnu   acwht

_____   _____   _____   _____

E Listen and chant. Then read.

The chick can catch a bug for lunch.

Unit 4 35

sh ch tch ph wh

A Listen and learn.

p h o n e

p h

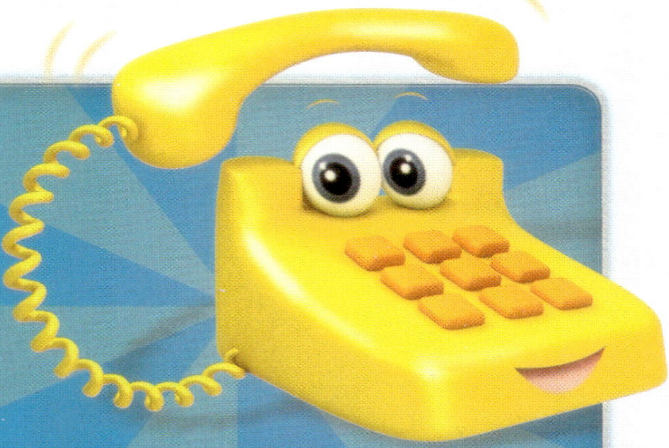

w h a l e

w h

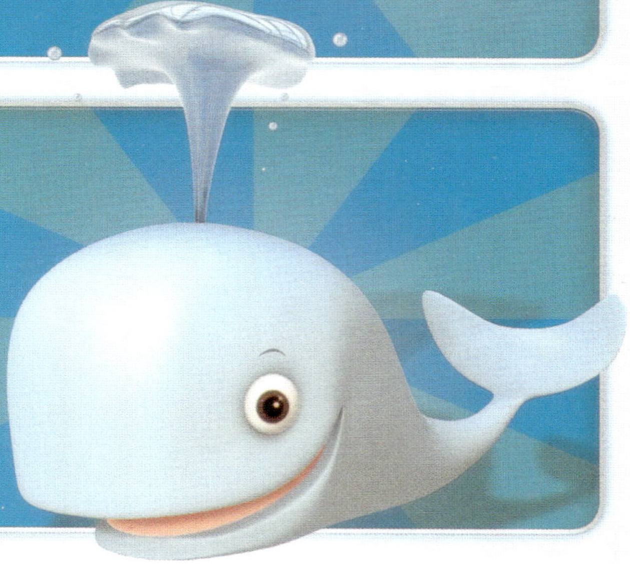

B Listen, point, and read.

1. 2. 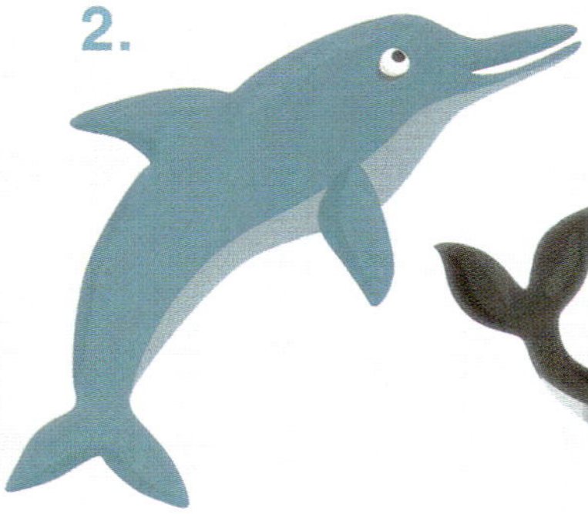 3. 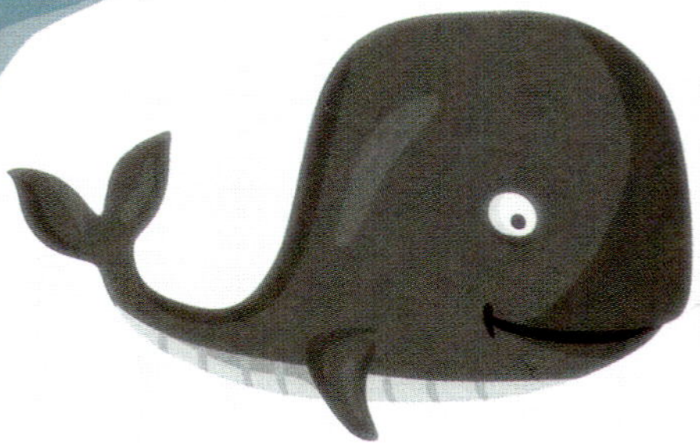 4.

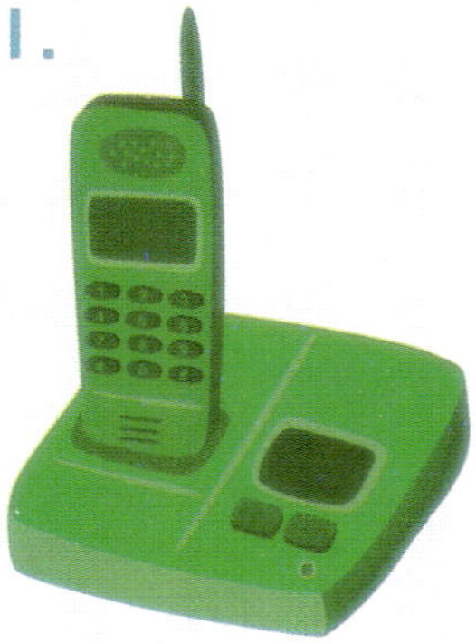

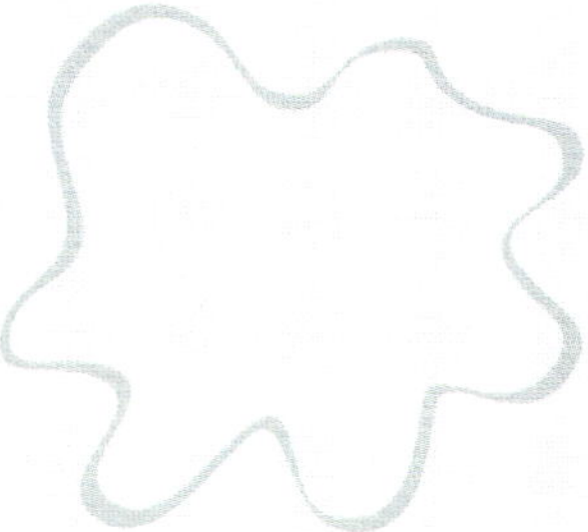

phone   dolphin   whale   white

sh ch tch ph wh

A Listen and write.

sh | ch | tch

ph | wh

Now try these!

Listen and circle.

Were you right?

1. ch / fl ___ eck
2. cl / wh ___ ip
3. ph / ch ___ ase
4. sh / dr ___ op
5. hi / di ___ tch
6. da / ca ___ sh

Story

B Look and listen. Read along. 🔊 64

Dolphin Bay

Brad and his family live on Dolphin Bay. They play catch on the beach and look for shells.

Brad's mom works on a big ship. She uses a net to catch fish.

His dad trains dolphins. People come to see them swim.

Brad works on the bay, too. Today, he sees a white whale! It's fun to live on Dolphin Bay.

New words: Brad family beach trains people
Sight words: works them today

Review 2

sm sn sp sw st sh ch tch ph wh

A Look and listen. Sing along.

Song

Come under the sea with me.
Let's see what we can see.
An old ship and lots of shells,
All red and yellow and blue.
You can catch a crab for me,
And I can catch a fish for you.

Come under the sea with me.
Let's see what we can see.
We can stop and look at a big, white whale
And see it swim away.
We can find a snake with a spot on his tail.
See the dolphins smile and play.

B Do the puzzle.

x	r	f	y	m	x	m	y	w	g	i	q
a	h	y	e	w	h	a	l	e	k	w	f
s	k	r	r	i	o	l	t	e	s	t	y
t	s	s	u	n	g	i	f	v	n	b	s
w	t	m	t	l	s	p	o	t	a	v	h
a	f	i	s	h	e	f	a	q	k	g	i
t	m	l	m	x	n	d	d	w	e	q	p
c	d	e	c	m	b	s	t	o	p	p	r
h	k	l	h	u	l	s	p	z	c	n	e
c	b	g	q	n	s	w	i	m	s	r	e

Review 2 | 41

sm sn sp sw st sh ch tch ph wh

C Listen and circle. 🎧 66

1.
ch ph sp

2.
sw st sm

3.
sh tch ch

4.
sh sw tch

5.
wh st sn

6.
sm ph sp

D Match and write.

1. sm——ing
   sw——oke

   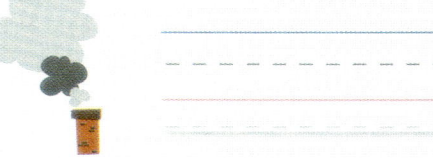

2. lun——ch
   bru——sh

   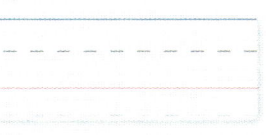

3. wh——ite
   ph——one

   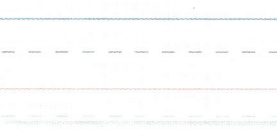

4. st——oon
   sp——amp

   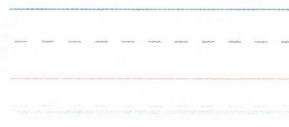

Review 2

sl dr tr sm sn sp sw st

Unit 5 — voiced th, unvoiced th, ck, qu

A Listen and learn. *disc 2 · 02*

this

t h

B Listen, point, and read. *disc 2 · 03*

1.
this

2.
that

3.
mother

4.
father

C Listen and circle.

1. father   mother
2. this   white
3. this   that
4. tree   mother

D Read and check.

1. ☐ This is my mother.
   ☐ This is my father.
2. ☐ This is my mother.
   ☐ That is my mother.
3. ☐ That is my father.
   ☐ This is my father.
4. ☐ That is my mother.
   ☐ That is my father.

E Listen and chant. Then read.

This is my father, and that is my mother.

Unit 5 45

voiced th unvoiced th ck qu

A Listen and learn. disc 2 06

three

t h

B Listen, point, and read. disc 2 07

1.
three

2.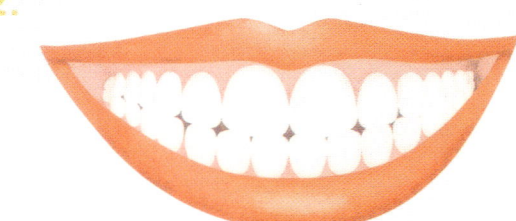
teeth

3.
think

4.
bath

voiced th unvoiced th ck qu

A Listen and learn. disc 2 / 11

d u c k

c k

q u e e n

q u

B Listen, point, and read. disc 2 / 12

1. duck
2. rocket
3. queen
4. quilt

Unit 5

 sn
 sp
 sw
 st
 sh
 ch
 tch
ph
w

voiced th **unvoiced** th ck qu

A Read and write.

mother queen bath that think this
duck father rocket teeth three quilt

voiced th

unvoiced th

ck

qu

Now try these! Listen, unscramble, and write. disc 2 · 15

Were you right?

1. orrhbte
2. hyte
3. hnit
4. mhat
5. csosk
6. iuqz

Story

B Look and listen. Read along. disc 2 / 16

Meet My Family

Hi, I'm Dale Duck. That is my father. He likes to bake cakes.

This is my mother. She likes to make quilts. When she sees a crocodile, she makes a loud quack!

That is my brother. He's a chick. He takes a bath with his toy rocket.

This is my family. One, two, three. I love my family, and they love me.

New words: meet   Dale   loud   quack   love
Sight words: when   brother   he's   toy   one   two

Unit 6 — ng nk nd nt lt mp

A Listen and learn. *disc 2 • 17*

k i n g
n g

b a n k
n k

B Listen, point, and read. *disc 2 • 18*

1. king
2. long
3. bank
4. pink

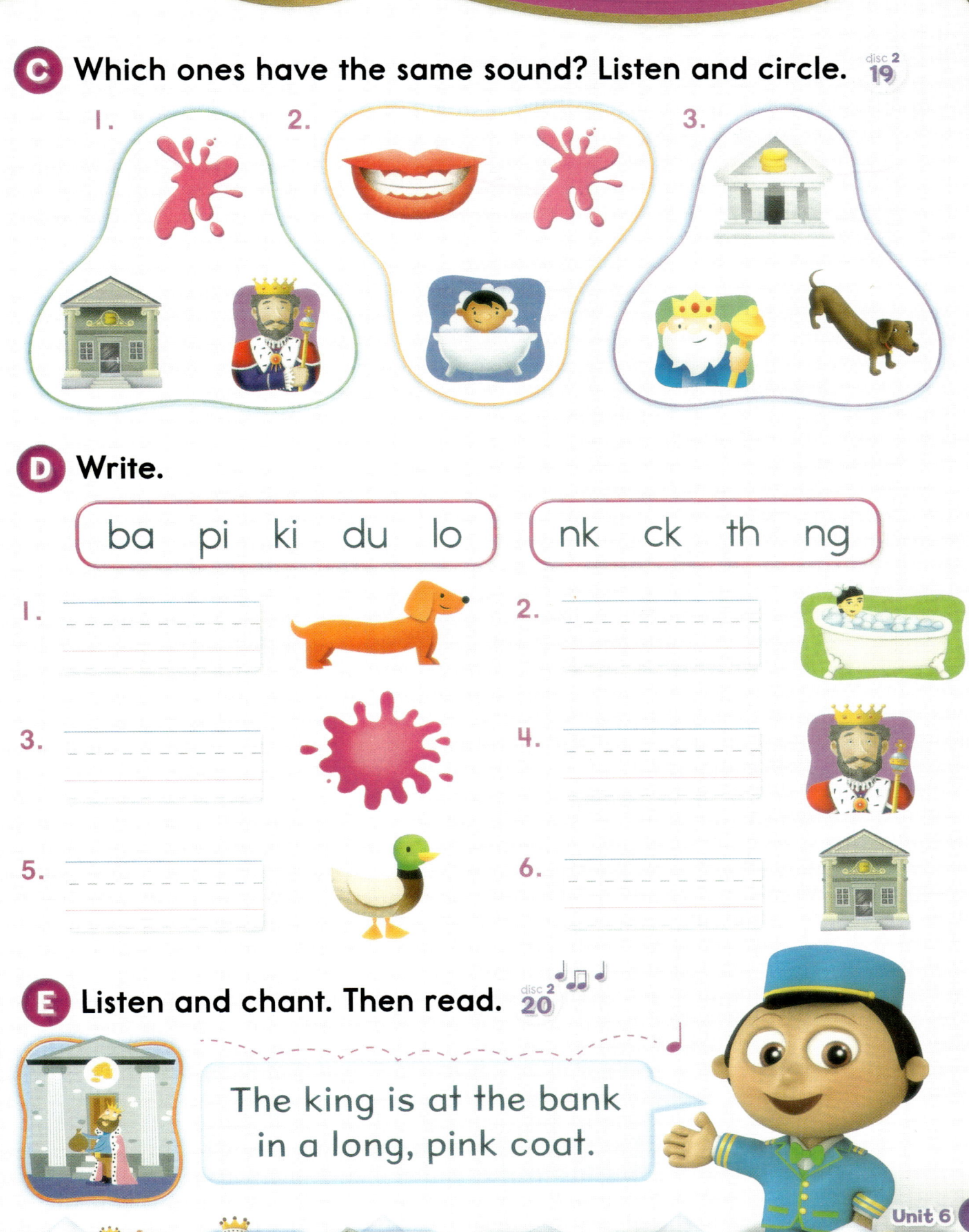

ng nk nd nt lt mp

A Listen and learn.

n + d = nd

wind

n + t = nt

tent

B Listen, point, and read.

1. wind
2. hand
3. tent
4. paint

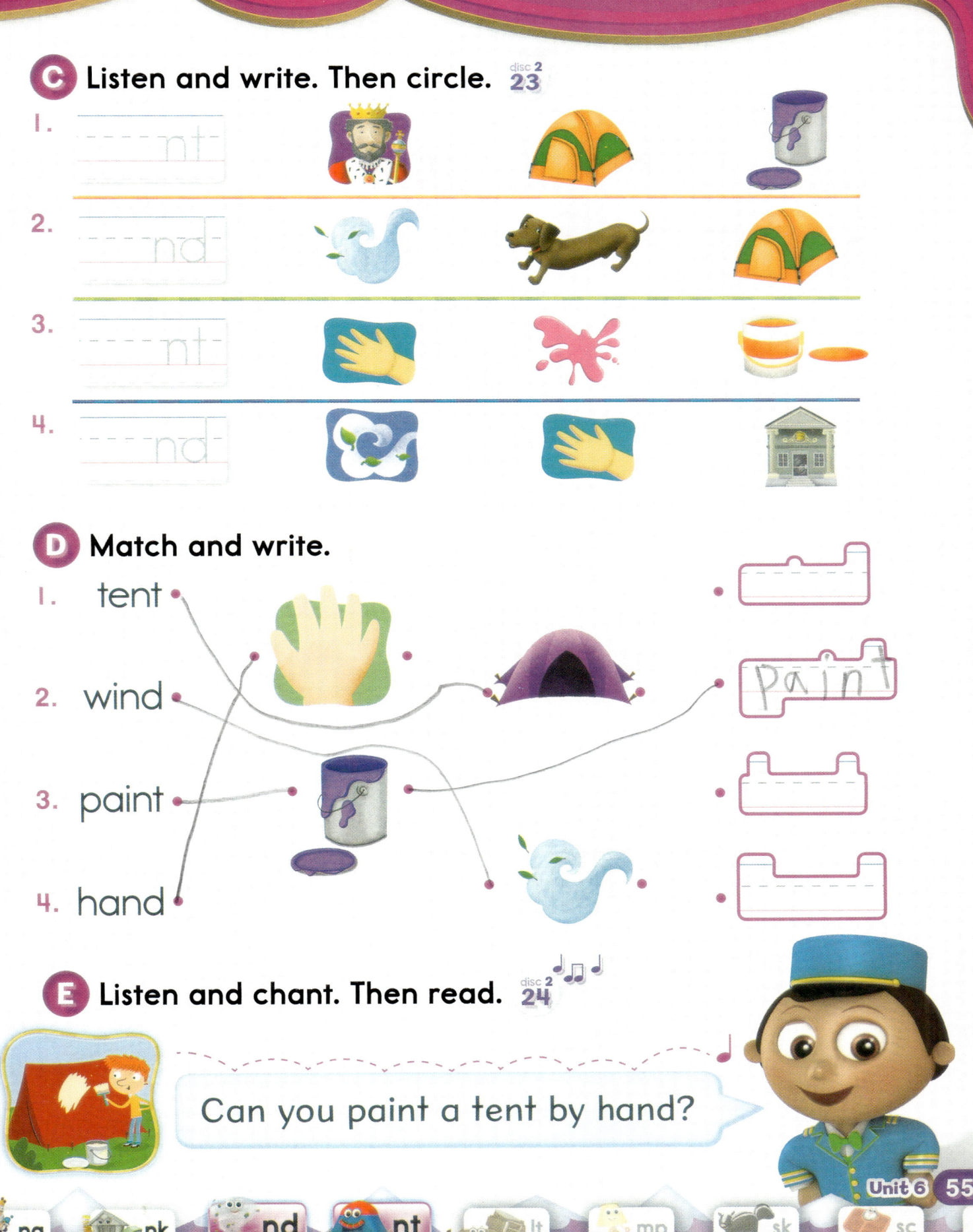

ng nk nd nt lt mp

A Listen and learn.

l + t = lt

belt

m + p = mp

lamp

B Listen, point, and read.

1. belt   2. adult   3. lamp   4. camp

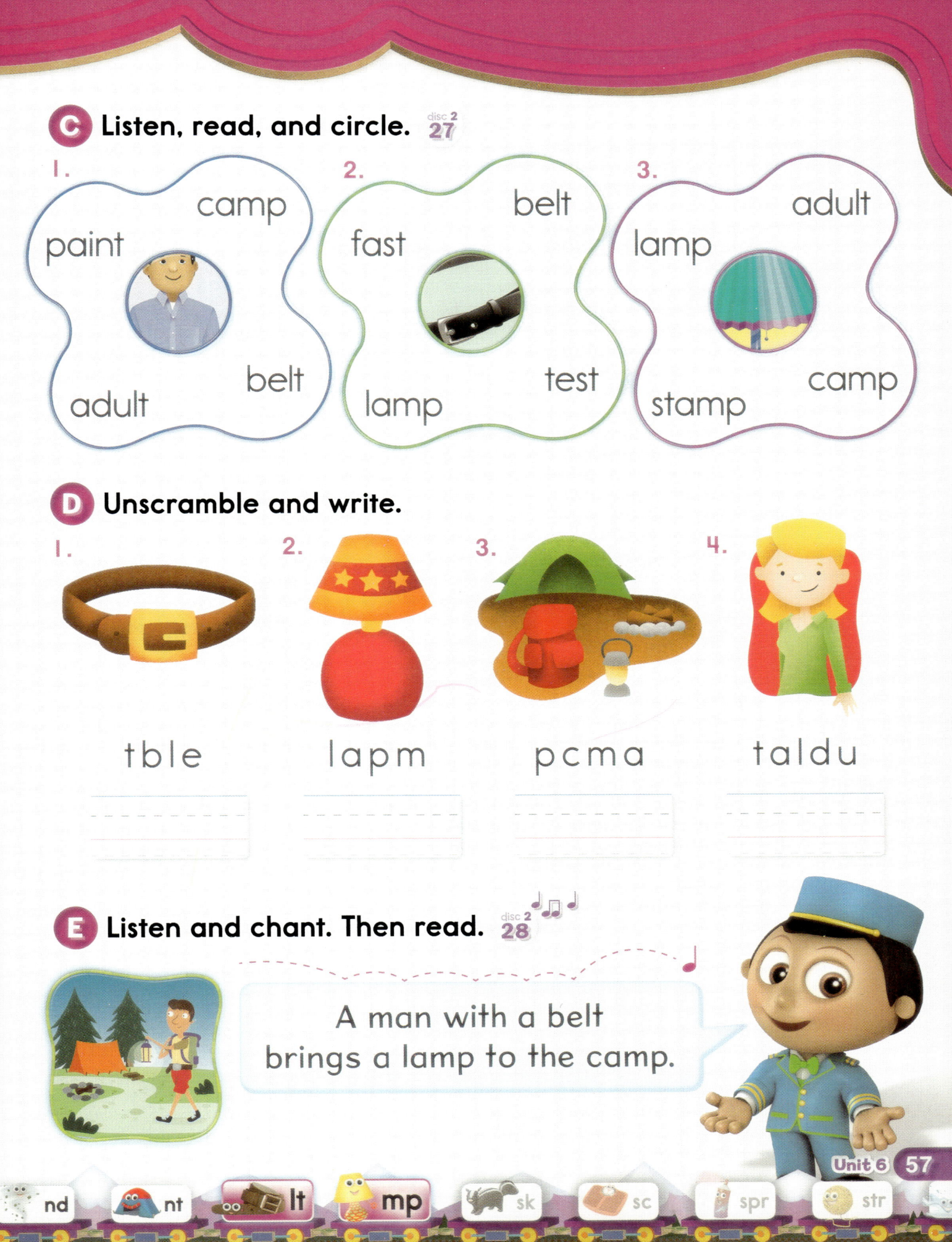

ng nk nd nt lt mp

A Listen and write. disc 2 29

| ng | nk | nd |
| nt | lt | mp |

Now try these! Listen and circle. disc 2 30

Were you right?

1. cha nt / pla
2. wi ng / si
3. si nk / li
4. ra mp / da
5. ba nd / la
6. me lt / pe

B Look and listen. Read along.

My Picture

I can paint a picture by hand.

I paint grass and a tree. I paint the sky, too. The grass is green, and the sky is blue.

I paint a king with a belt and a queen in a long, pink robe. Then I paint a camp with three tents and a lamp.

I paint the wind. It blows the camp. It blows the king and queen, too. Oh, no!

New words: robe   blows   Sight words: picture   by

Review 3

voiced unvoiced
th th ck qu ng nk nd nt lt mp

A Look and listen. Sing along.

Song

This is a picture of summer camp,
My family, and me.
This is my father. That is my mother.
This is my brother. I'm nine. He's three.

We make our food with a spoon and a pot.
We use a lamp for light.
We take our big, pink quilt to bed
And sleep in a tent at night.

B Do the puzzle.

1. 
2. 
3. 
4. 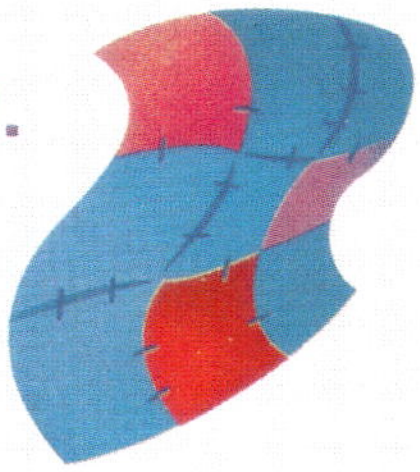
5.

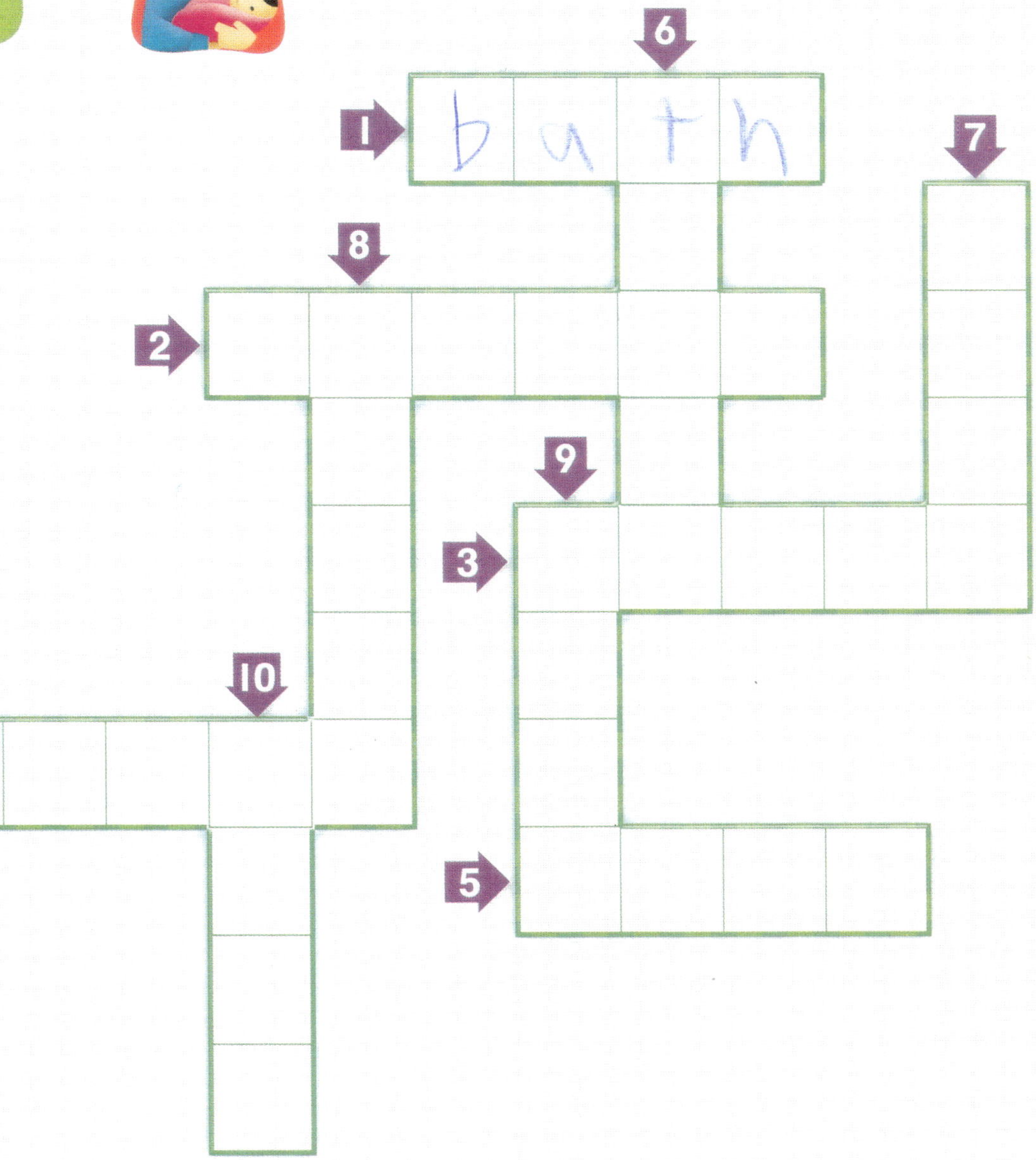

1 → b a t h

6.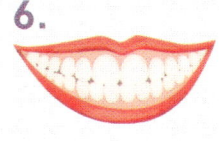
7.
8.
9.
10.

voiced unvoiced
th th ck qu ng nk nd nt lt mp

C Listen and circle. disc 2 · 33

1.
nk mp lt

2.
nk ck th

3.
th nd nt

4.
qu th nt

5.
nd mp ng

6.
th qu ck

D Match and write.

1. ki──nk
   pi──ng

2. be──mp
   ca──lt

3. qu──een
   th──ree

4. wi──nd
   te──nt

Unit 7   sk sc spr str spl squ

A Listen and learn. disc 2 34

s + k = sk

skunk

s + c = sc

scale

B Listen, point, and read. disc 2 35

1.
2.
3.
4.

skunk   de**sk**   **sc**ale   **sc**hool

C Listen, read, and match. 🔊 disc 2 · 36

1. school •
   scale •

2. • scale
   • duck

3. watch •
   desk •

4. • school
   • skunk

D Read and write.

1. I use a _____ at school.

2. The man stands on the _____.

3. This _____ is black and white.

4. I see my friends at _____.

E Listen and chant. Then read. 🎵 disc 2 · 37

A skunk is under the desk at school.

Unit 7 65

 lt  mp  sk  sc  spr  str spl squ

sk sc spr str spl squ

A Listen and learn.

s + p + r = spr

spray

s + t + r = str

string

B Listen, point, and read.

1.  spray
2.  spring
3.  string
4.  strong

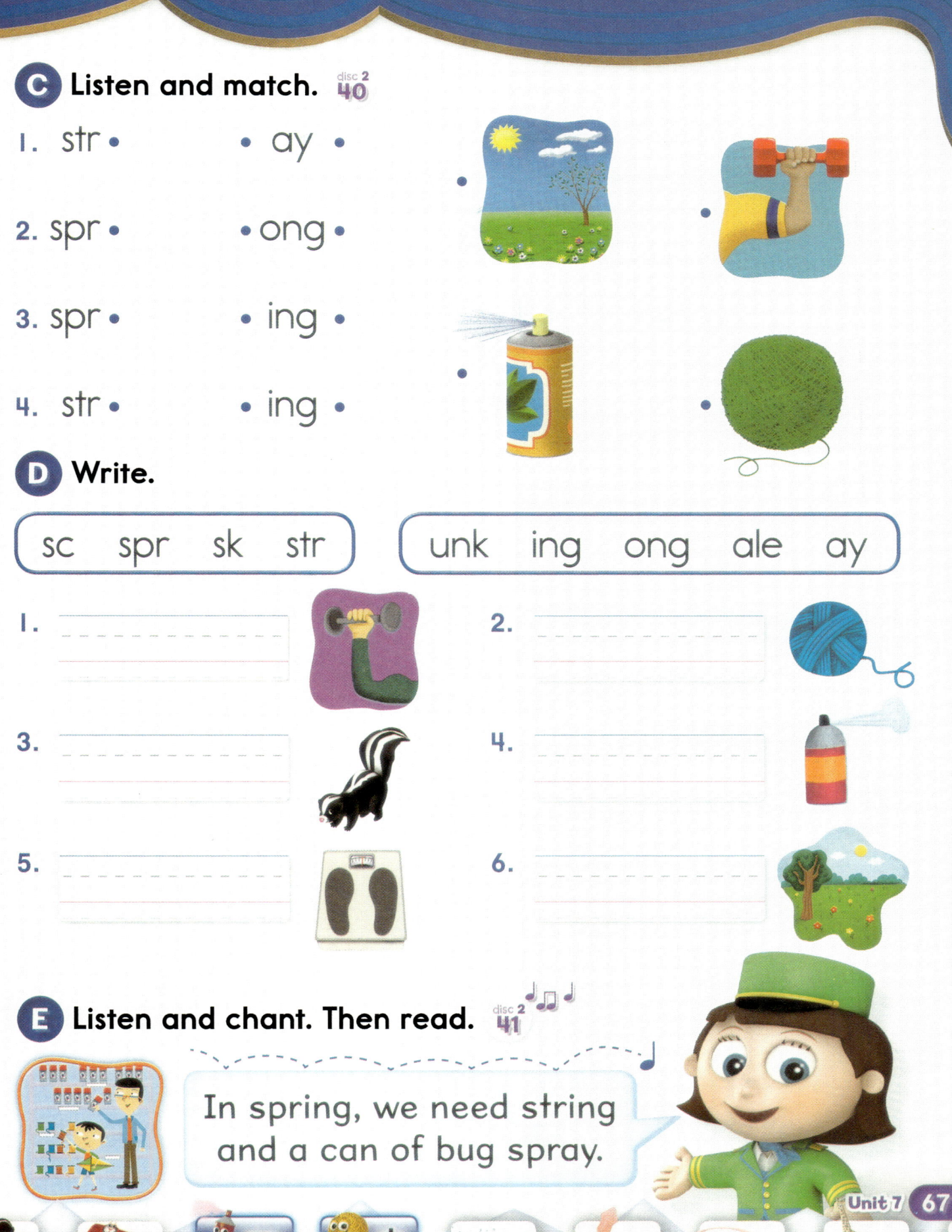

sk sc spr str **spl squ**

A Listen and learn.

s + p + l = spl

splash

s + qu = squ

squid

B Listen, point, and read.

1. splash
2. splint
3. squid
4. square

C. Listen and number. Then match.

splint ☐   squid ☐   splash ☐   square ☐

D. Listen and circle. Then write.

1. spl — ash / int

2. squ — are / id

3. str — ong / ing

4. spr — ay / ing

5. spl — ash / int

6. squ — id / are

E. Listen and chant. Then read.

Nine big squids splash and play in the bay.

sk sc spr str spl squ

A Read and write.

splash   strong   desk   squid   string   scale
spray   skunk   splint spring square   school

sk

sc

spr

str

spl

squ

Now try these! Listen, unscramble, and write. Were you right?

1. psik

2. casn

3. irtspn

4. erttes

5. stlip

6. aqksue

Story

B Look and listen. Read along.

A Bad Skunk

It's a pretty spring day. The squid kids are in school.

A skunk jumps into the sea. Splash! He wants to catch the squids!

The kids swim under their desks. They spray black ink. The skunk can't see!

The squid teacher is strong. He picks up the skunk and puts him on the grass. The skunk is sorry!

New words: bad   teacher   sorry
Sight words: pretty   jumps   into   can't   picks

Unit 8 — soft c, soft g, voiced s

A Listen and learn. *disc 2 49*

r i c e

c

B Listen, point, and read. *disc 2 50*

1.

   rice

2.

   city

3.

   ice cream

4.

   cell phone

C Which ones have the same sound? Listen and circle. disc 2 51

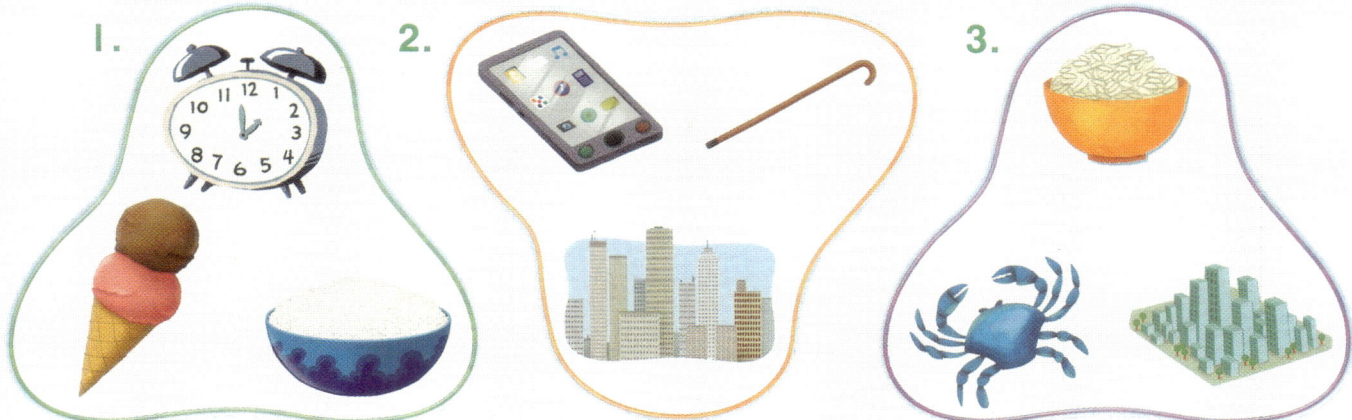

D Match and write.

1. city   2. rice   3. ice cream   4. cell phone

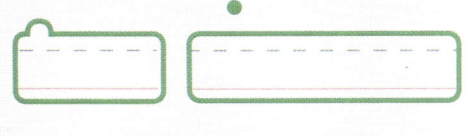 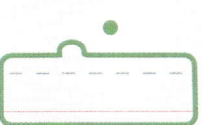 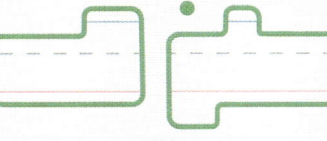

E Listen and chant. Then read. disc 2 52

People in the city like rice and ice cream.

spl   squ   c   g   s

soft c soft g voiced s

A Listen and learn. *disc 2 53*

giraffe

g

B Listen, point, and read. *disc 2 54*

1. giraffe

2. orange

3. giant

4. cage

 nd  nt  lt  mp  sk  sc  spr str  sp

A Listen and learn.

r o s e

s

B Listen, point, and read.

1.

rose

2.

jeans

3.

cheese

4.

legs

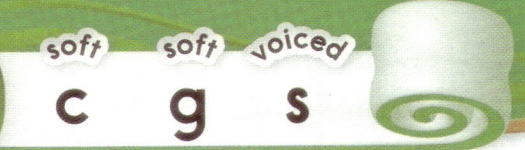

soft c   soft g   voiced s

A Listen and write. disc 2 61

soft c	soft g	voiced s

 Listen and circle. disc 2 62

1. g ym / g el
2. hand s / tub s
3. c ircle / c ircus

Were you right?

B Look and listen. Read along.

Jim Giant

Jim Giant lives in a city. He has a big cell phone and huge blue jeans.

His lunch is huge, too! Jim eats ten plates of rice, nine oranges, a pot of cheese, and one small ice cream cone.

He has a pet giraffe named Spot. Spot has a long nose and very long legs. He likes to eat roses.

"No, Spot! Don't eat that rose!"

New words: Jim huge named   Sight words: very

Review 4

sk sc spr str spl squ c(soft) g(soft) s(voiced)

A Look and listen. Sing along. *disc 2 64*

Song

I live in the city, and I have a giraffe.
He sleeps in a big, square cage.

I ride him to school. He's very strong.
He's orange and black, and his legs are long.
"Oh, no," says my teacher. "I'm sorry.
 Your huge giraffe can't come in."

So I tie my giraffe to the gate.
From my desk, I see him wait
And wait and wait all day.

Then we eat ice cream and play!
We eat ice cream and play.

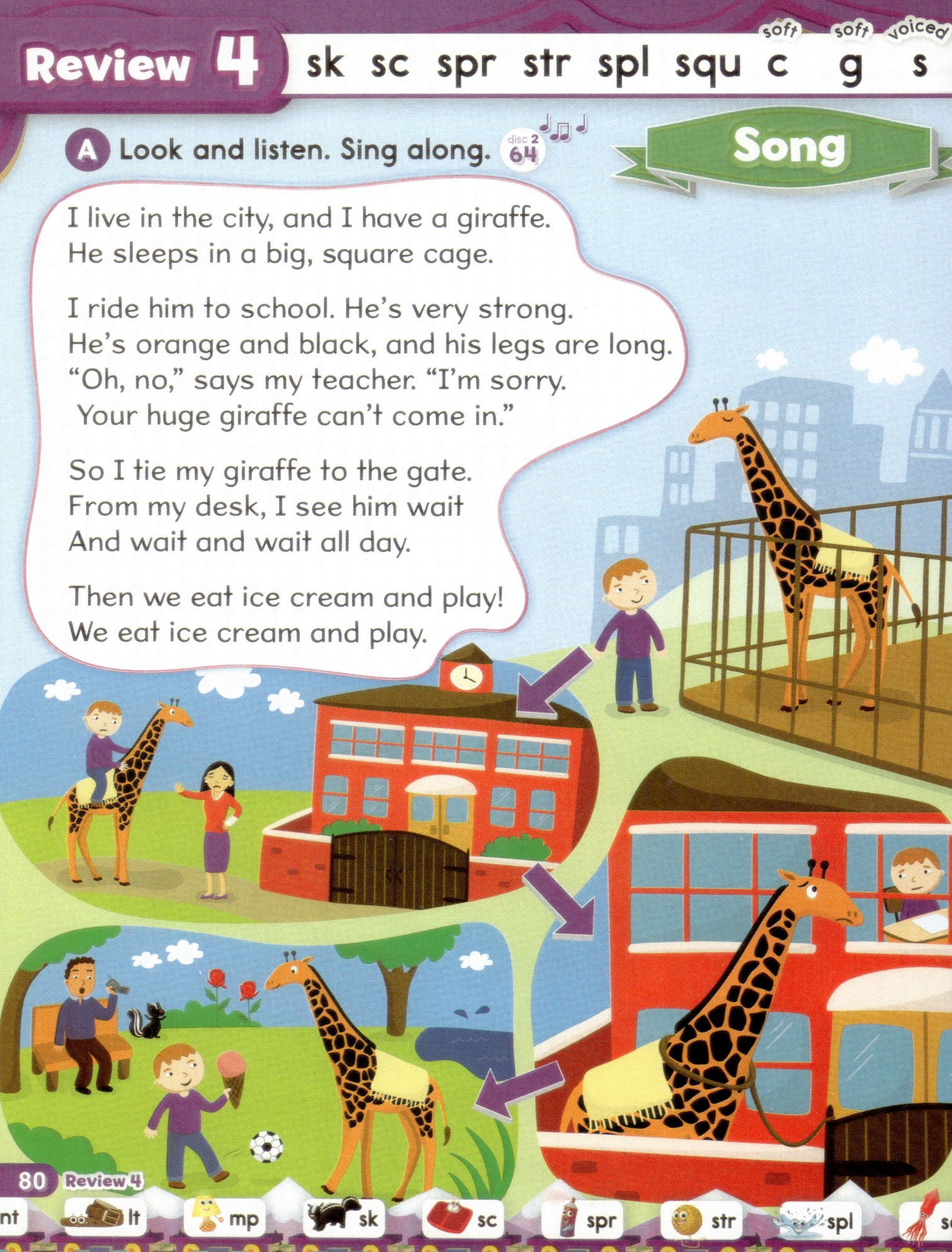

B Do the puzzle.

g	c	b	h	d	x	r	r	l	o	l	b
y	c	r	v	k	z	m	o	o	y	j	r
p	q	i	c	u	k	l	s	r	g	r	u
s	h	c	v	j	b	j	e	a	n	s	n
k	c	e	l	l	p	h	o	n	e	l	y
i	a	i	g	d	t	m	m	g	f	f	c
t	n	n	n	c	e	l	l	e	g	s	i
b	g	i	a	n	t	t	q	e	i	o	t
p	i	k	c	a	g	e	o	v	b	h	y
u	b	h	f	w	a	i	o	d	e	s	k

Review 4 81

sk sc spr str spl squ c g s
                              soft soft voiced

C Listen and circle. disc 2 · 65

1.
   c   s   g

2.
   spr   sc   spl

3.
   s   g   c

4.
   spr   spl   str

5.
   c   sk   squ

6.
   g   str   s

D Match and write.

1. spl — int
   squ — id
       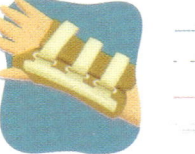

2. sc — ong
   str — hool

3. squ — ale
   sc — are
      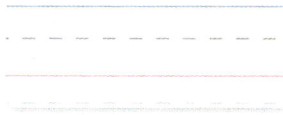   

4. str — ing
   spr — ay

82 Review 4

Picture Dictionary

Aa

Bb

Cc

Ss

Student Cards

1. black	2. blanket	3. clock	4. club
5. broom	6. bride	7. crab	8. crocodile
9. fly	10. flag	11. globe	12. glass
13. frog	14. Friday	15. green	16. grass

17 plate	18 play	19 slide	20 sleep
21 drum	22 dress	23 truck	24 tree
25 smile	26 smoke	27 snake	28 snow
29 spoon	30 spot	31 swing	32 swim

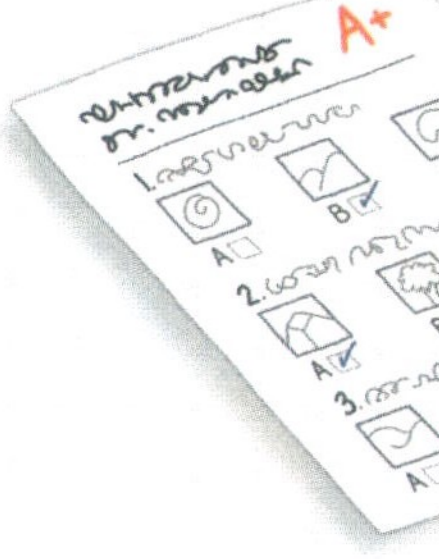

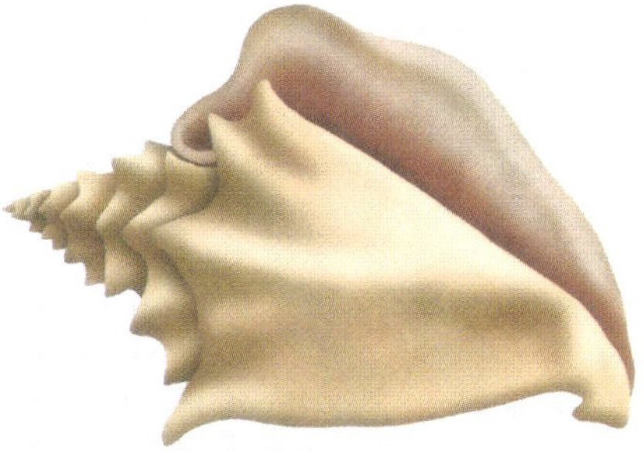

33 stop	34 test	35 stamp	36 fast
37 shell	38 fish	39 ship	40 brush
41 chick	42 lunch	43 watch	44 catch
45 phone	46 dolphin	47 whale	48 white

49 this	50 that	51 mother	52 father
53 three	54 teeth	55 think	56 bath
57 duck	58 rocket	59 queen	60 quilt
61 king	62 long	63 bank	64 pink

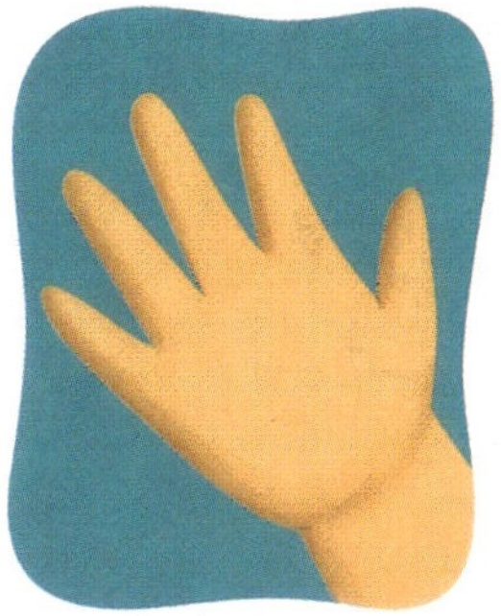

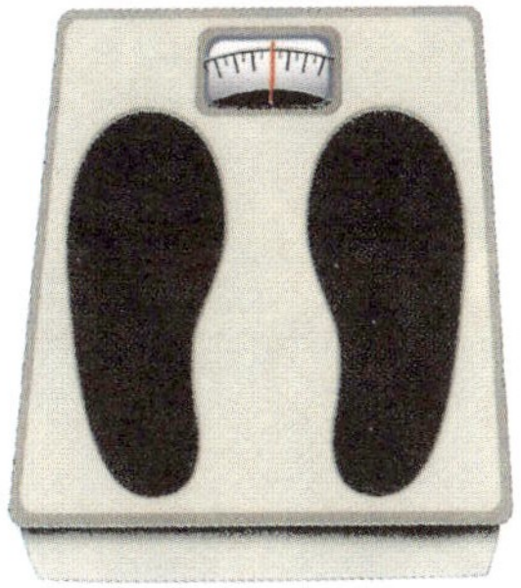

65 wind	66 hand	67 tent	68 paint
69 belt	70 adult	71 lamp	72 camp
73 skunk	74 desk	75 scale	76 school
77 spray	78 spring	79 string	80 strong

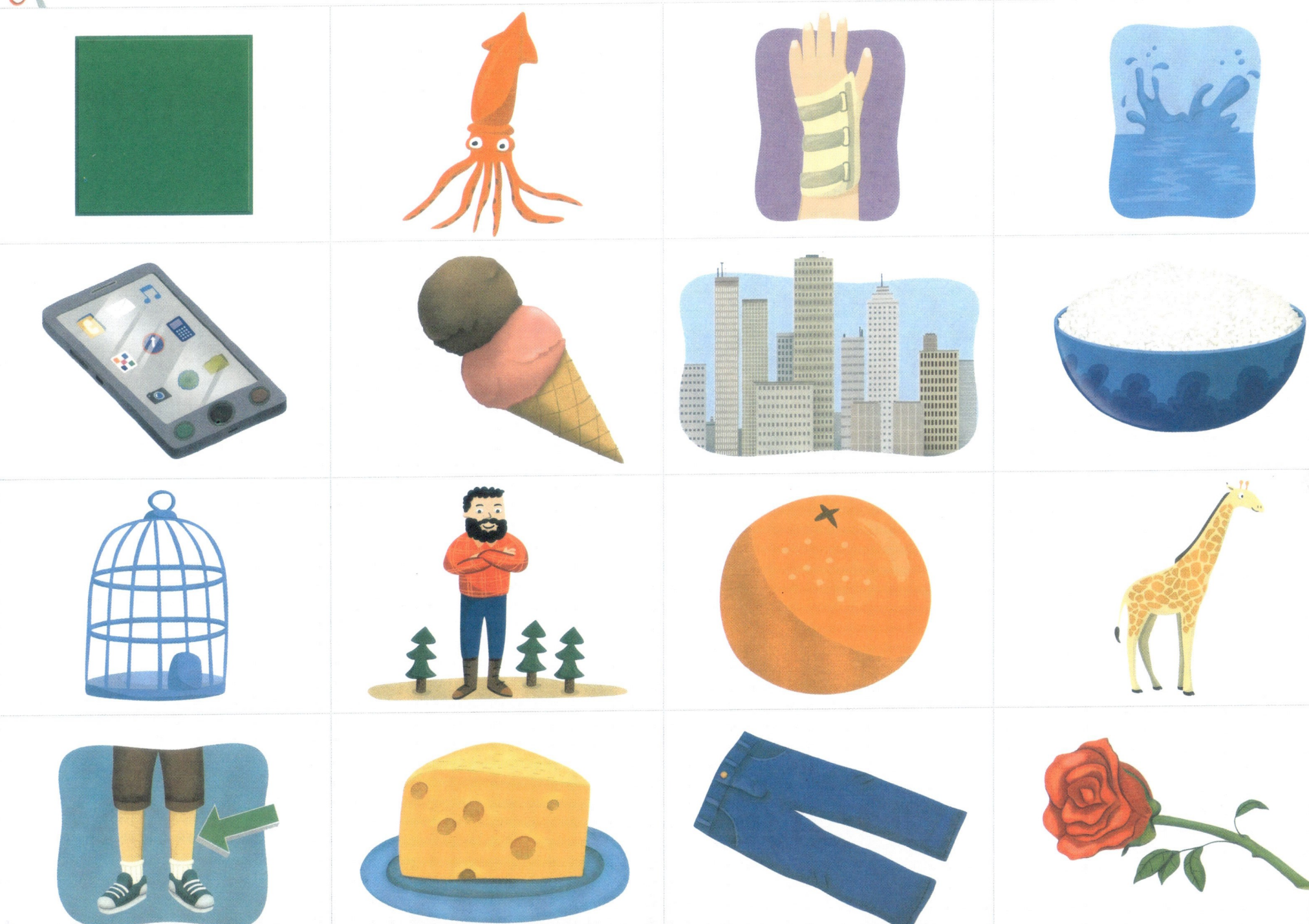

81 splash	82 splint	83 squid	84 square
85 rice	86 city	87 ice cream	88 cell phone
89 giraffe	90 orange	91 giant	92 cage
93 rose	94 jeans	95 cheese	96 legs

Congratulations!

This certifies that

_____

has successfully completed

Oxford Phonics World 4
Consonant Blends

on _____.

Signature _____

Date _____